SHEARSMAN

99 & 100

SUMMER 2014

EDITOR
TONY FRAZER

Shearsman magazine is published in the United Kingdom by
Shearsman Books Ltd
50 Westons Hill Drive | Emersons Green | BRISTOL BS16 7DF

Editor: Tony Frazer

Registered office: 30-31 St James Place, Mangotsfield, Bristol BS16 9JB
(this address not for correspondence)
www. shearsman.com
ISBN 978-1-84861-333-1
ISSN 0260-8049

Acknowledgements

The poems by Christopher Middleton in this issue have already appeared in the
author's *Collected Later Poems* (Carcanet, Manchester, 2014), the publisher having
beaten us to the punch. Please buy the book.

Subscriptions and single copies

Current subscriptions—covering two double-issues, with an average length of 108
pages—cost £14 for delivery to U.K. addresses, £17 for the rest of Europe (including
the Republic of Ireland), and £19 for the rest of the world. Longer subscriptions
may be had for a pro-rata higher payment. North American customers will find
that buying single copies from online retailers in the U.S.A. will be cheaper than
subscribing. £19 equated to just over $31 at the time we went to press, and single
copies cost $14 retail in the U.S.A. The reason for this discrepancy is that overseas
postage rates in the U.K. have been rising rapidly, whereas copies of the magazine
are printed in the U.S.A. to meet local demand from online retailers there, and thus
avoid the transatlantic journey.

Back issues from n° 63 onwards (uniform with this issue)—cost £8.50 / $14 through
retail outlets. Single copies can be ordered for £8.50, post-free, direct from the press,
through the Shearsman online store, or from bookstores in the U.K. and the U.S.A.
Issues of the old pamphlet-style version of the magazine, from issue n° 1 to 62,
may be had for £3 each, direct from the press, where they are still available, but
contact us for prices for a full, or partial, run.

Submissions

Shearsman operates a submissions-window system, whereby submissions are only
accepted during the months of March and September, when selections are
made for the October and April issues, respectively. Submissions may be sent
by mail or email, but email attachments—other than PDFs—are not accepted.
We aim to respond within 3 months of the window's closure.

CONTENTS

CHRISTOPHER MIDDLETON

Eurydice Perceived

> '...the singing insect whose records
> are inscribed in our coal-seams.'
> J.-H. Fabre

What if I never again for once could see
her strict small face brighten to a gift
What if I tipped the attic windows open
and never woke again to birdsong rushing up
Torched by curiosity even as I caught my breath
I let the forelock of a moment slip
so rare a time that idled is

A moment captured strikes you unawares
but grows a form gradually in afterthought

Wait: in immediacy akin to music
unlike music the moments change their form
And even music loved but heard distractedly
a ton of times weighs never quite the same

So in a shroud the figure lifted
                        now most herself
shocked by the light out there incipient
her gaunt features were shaping to smile

What end then spells out the stuffs in variance?
What were the words that came to grandfather?
It is the quality of the affection
that carves in a mind the trace...

I trace values on a map until the end
Let the quality, gods, of my affection
go deep as the clarity of grandfather's eyes

When memory in a moment shifts its parallel
I'll see and hear again re-opening the question

Even if Eros with a tusk scatters her garden
O predecessors you who teach restraint
with the grasshopper's voice our whispers blend
yours console in the shadow of her pergolas

Our Rain Crow

'Car no chanta auzels ni piula…'
—Arnaut Daniel

How apt of this rain crow
as rain came pattering down
for our flowers on the fresh grave
to hoot from his haunted orchard
sotto voce twice.

Then a wave had crested, giving rise
to fields of force; foaming vortices
carpenter the island of Phaeacia;
liquid eye-beams, Greek and chisel
carve to measure the finest of ships.

'Some few accustomed forms,
the absolute unimportant':
thus E.P. on a distinct slant
(still at an early age)
plotting some real connections.

So it is, here for the oldest folks
who still can hobble by,
there is a dangerous dog proclaiming
his Ah Ah Ah. One rough day's ride
and the sea crashes ashore.

I see my orchard gone for good.
Antiquated, for a moment
reasonably trees revive. One single twig
or two blossoming would cradle
a twitter of linnets. Soon
the punctual cuckoo too must croak. If
a cherry reddens,

it is for air, also the choir
far out in France at first light
let fly with one voice overtopping all;
yes, in the accustomed form,
it was the oriole, his folded fluting
for dear life I now recall.

What sense do I make, shedding this skin?
Memory, had you none tougher hidden?
Ancient shipyard fantasm,
fantasm orchard, sacred ground;
the texture puzzles, there is disbelief.
I do perceive it, past denying
pedestals to my words; to our crow its rain.

*[Note: Rain Crow is the by-name, current in rustic
Central Texas, for the yellow-billed cuckoo.]*

The Path Long Overgrown

What is this reckless
little thing
a magnet far

swept back wings
a tiny Concord

and a cat's
crooked whisker
sprouts

out of each nostril
of the pointed nose

Where the wings widen
a lightning bolt
bridges them

not a sound
one scorching zig

zag
long a portent
in these Navajo lands

and of what ganglion
turning and turning

a paroxysm,
the gaze unstilled
this fascination

vaporous cage fixed
for the stiffening
animal and petty

intelligence starved
by the abstract—

Look now, she will sing,
how the mobs get going
daily quicker footstep

of old, cottages to thatch,
a soul within and secret

divine things
always
further on.

Dilemma after a Serious Injury

'All mere complexities…'

The cocks of Hades, even mute,
Still they inform against me.

My birds will make me better
The wren will call to hear from me
Sing for my supper; mockingbird

Just now I have to call the landlady
And tell her how I decide.

I could hail the locomotive horn
Otherwise, after midnight.

.

PETER RILEY

from The Mayroyd Notebook

Three turns of the concrete road up through the woods,
you sense warmth from the valley below: voices,
chimneys, shopping, a silent and invisible wall
cloistering hope and resignation. I have brought
my ignorance and wordlessness up the hillside in spite
of sciatica, to plant them in last year's leaf mould,
where the trees cease the stonewalled pastures begin
and after the last wall open moorland, above all else,
the wind tugs the heather stalk, the wilderness rhetoric
flatters my ignorance and a glance back opens
an archive of industrial prints, of belonging,
inward-facing houses, the old fellow takes
his usual lunch. Why must we say goodbye to all that?
Because it was never there, we made a show out of it,
a show to show what we are, to show us at our best,
desire in meadow and stream, local voice
vocal choice as if stable.

   Round the last corner the late sun
   smites the hill slopes tumble
   out of the horizon a white horse
   takes the full slant of light a
   wordlessness of babies resounds
   across the world and the show
   must go on, it *must* go on.

MARY LEADER

Crone Cards
Series II

1.
You, Polymath, come, tattooed with the word
"Strange." Not the words "The interior of
The person," where, according to Bacon,
Words "come from." Me, I look to the margins:
A shoal of chevrons, a staircase of curves,
Near words. There's "mystical" for you, sir:
Ruins of sulfur- or mustard-colored clay
Walls, writ upon with shadows not quite black.
Relief. Now you've called off the search, read me
As inner/outer, as alchemical.
Meanwhile I putter, which constitutes urge
Without desire, cogitation without
Heat. I shall wash in tepid, rinse in cool,
My soap attesting to roses and rue.

2.
Even when I understand how you, care-
Fully, use a word as a term of art—
A technical term—in physics, painting,
Philosophy, I snatch it, plug it in-
To the socket of the quotidian
As if it meant that too. Or worse, instead
Of. You say "field" as in realm of action
And thought, then I turn around, fill it per-
Versely with Queen-Anne's-Lace Milkweed, Monarch
Butterflies and patches of mud. The best
Light I can put on this violence is
Calling it interference as you
Elucidate the concept(s). Forgive me.
I cannot thank you enough for your works.

3.

One needs some kind of a crest in order
To lead soldiers into battle or send
Them into battle but not to lead them
Wending to where the access road ceases
And the war zone recedes, spared by dint of
Desertion, attention turned to trees and
Eventually back to tables bright
With color. (All heresies, so saith
Jerome, come from women.) Autumn trees, like
Hung tapestries, done up in fading pomp.
Not that I damn, per se, Jerome's busy
Solitude. Afternoons, right where the sun
Shines in from, casement to flagstone, the saint's
Lion mellows out, warm and protected.

4.

O shapes who rode with the spur, and the rust,
The washing damp on the rocks, how is it
The field must have been seen, how it is cupped
Forearms beneath the shape of the hill, how
Is it in need of explaining, how such
Brimmed forearms kept filling; who is it
Is filling the skim and sway in the hill?
The line of your man's hand points to those
Who cannot hide. Are you Don Quixote
Who rode out wing whip of air explaining
The ground, but not when it is as damp as
Washing, how it is it offers the sun
Dew, condensation, the sky bent over
Whom it is that the forearms belong

5.

I will not be pure, nor purity bring,
The next time I revisit light to cope
With the world's lost hope, not be narrow as
Before, I promise. I will go, open,
Unfrightened by night, accustomed to
The dark, as I am, as it is. By day,
Even so, I will advise my neighbors
About the little crops if not against
The fallacy that toil outlasts death. Send
Oats, peas, beans, and barley in the sudden
Spring; give them mirth if not diversion. Then
Winter, rotate, a fresh welcome, ye wheat
And ye rye. Farewell, dear Arcadia,
Where the airs mingle, glory: we too, here.

6.

Rich already is my life, and it means.
Can it mean value added tax that I'll
See you, Double Amphibrach, for the last
Time at some staid meeting in Stewart Hall?
Will you or will I mind it that nothing,
Well, nothing very personal, transpired
Between us? Come next blossoms, you might learn,
From a list-serve memo, I'm bending with
The remover to remove. A world dark
Office evening, the sole scholar present
That time of a Friday night, I twirled out
Eleven silver spokes from your writing.
I wish that my spine would last a while yet,
Or collapse, right away, and finish me.

7.
Has not Gertrude Stein told us that "sugar
Is not a vegetable"? One summer
From now, or two, I plan to acquire at
My local craft-supply chain-store, twenty
Six-inch wan -plain wooden letters, paint them,
Each one different, naturally, yes, most
Decoratively! probably red and
Green predominating, spelling out Stein's
Sentence, of course left-to-right alignment,
Up there on the plate-rail in my kitchen.
What do you think? Calculate paisley shapes?
Vine-&-flower type things? Or some of each?
Concentric circles for the O in NOT?
Kandinsky's yellows, Klee's pinks, their tangents.

8.
Even in sere August, I am in love.
So many vine trumpeters, such casings
Of beetles, all that iridescence, what
Perfect accessories for my black veil!
Although I don't grow zinnias myself,
I remember zinnias, mixed colors
All marrying; they'd make quite a nice scarf.
Gradually, pasts return, small array,
Lovers, a few, I can name each. Sowers
Of drizzle visit me now. I would be
Clover, unshepherded, in this slight rain.
I see little, but eyes can easily
Be shut, unlike ears, wherein, days apart,
Someone seems to plant shallow sounds, for me.

9.
Yeah, this is the mania blurting. But
I know these are brilliant. Almost I think—
No, not true—they could tear either of us
In half. Split sun in the Icarus myth?
Precisely what was I wearing when you
First made eye contact with me at that first
(For me) "Primary Committee" meeting:
A stretch-lace purple shirt and a velvet
Taupe-brown jacket. I was the new-comer.
That was what? eight years ago. Old cycle,
It's re-begun? This semester, at that
Earliest of meetings, my wave to you
Was salute-like. I had on a business
Vest in navy, a simple pale green shell.

10.
Not that I don't still watch the main road for
The unanticipated arrival
Of a canon, riding "lik as he were
Wood" [mad] (Chaucer). I hold my own walking
Stick with handle facing forward, as learnt.
You rise close by, Man in the Moon, you check
The stars to make sure they're correct, wind them
If necessary. Your heart is human.
But I will probably never know what
Hurts you. The sunflowers back home, wild and
Rampant, make me cry. There were sunflowers,
Yes? when, as you put it, you were Russian.
What is your patronymic? Did someone
Call you Arkasha? Your brown eyes move me.

Su Fan Shan at Dajin Waterfall

She wades through the pool
towards the fall's clatter, each
dappled step deeper;
and the eye takes part in the
current's green ascent,
after its leap into space,
to lap her brown limbs,
like schoolboys in a classroom
hungry for knowledge—
shall we say of the language?
its many clauses
a lifting hem as one thing
follows another
into an opposite track,
changing the subject
from life's possibilities
to what they become,
just a matter of grammar
or a bird's chirrup
from the hollow of a rock.

Correspondances

Walls crumble in the wind and already
The blurred petals of birds in tumbling flight
Scud over the road like rags tugging free
From the structure. Incised in the surface
Some figure or script would draw you beneath
That when you try to decipher is gone;
Only attentive inwardness remains

And the greetings of correspondences,
A statue's discarded arm pulling down
About your shoulders the rustling water
Of burned leaves and the hum of bees looping
In emerald necklaces through the orchards.

What there is to reveal does not travel
Such pathways, unweave as you will the clue
Lizards leave, pore where the paws of squirrels
Pause or go the way that monkeys augur;
They only lead deeper into the maze
Where the muse's siren serenade is
The bullfrog's call that has your name by heart,
Not knowing you are nearby to hear it,
The day's reiteration of voices
Each with its own variation of air
No competition changes to coherence.
Dragons writhe round the newels as you walk,
Golden nymphs launch heavenwards from the lamps;
From the crook of trees and cracks in the wall
Orchids unfurl celestial garments.
Every trunk in the dry climate doubles
And then redoubles into a cloister,
Living pillars of confused utterance
Where perfumes, sounds and colours worship
The archetype's primitive completion.

Though the sum never adds up, yet counting
Continues, like a warbler wooing you
Over and over from the reeds: 'How do?'
And as promised it's there in the rhythm,
In the unmixed colours—arterial
Red, the sun's butter spread on still water,
The deep sky's sapphire at meridian.
But don't you hear instead the translation
Of rainfall into the mango's flavour

Strumming on glass like the stone's fibrous strands
Wreathing the cuspids in the mouth's rock pool?
Yet behind it the fruit's single sunburst
Insists it is greater than that mating
Flight of butterflies, 'how do?', that if you'd
Let them would dance your glance away again
Into the distance. Resist their allure.
All that remains is to straighten your back
And mount one by one then the waiting stairs
Anonymously into the thin air.

The Infinite Meeting

When the other two appeared
it was as if two nails
were slowly hammered upward
into the quivering noon.

A dipper of water was ready
in the shade of the well's parapet.

Wordlessly we offered
simple bread of the district,
having in common
only such language as gift,

aware that at such an hour
monks of the silent order walk.

Almost merging with its perch,
a crow on a bitter thorn
had paused in its pilgrimage,
our solitude's companion,

like a black crust shared,
a wine laid down in hope.

And of the four pairs of hands
busied there with the mundane
not one lifted on leaving,
so fast was our brotherhood

rooted in earth and sky
by our communion.

What parting is possible
when in the strict accounting
the wilderness demands
time is swept from its counter?

Even the dead we have buried
work to the surface like stones.

Vultures in a Classical Landscape

Old olive trees, their gnarled trunks
Wreathed into one, are niched with hollows
As if to enthrone the place's gods,
Who have preferred this pillared hillside
To a remote and flawless heaven.

None, climbing into the silence here,
Escapes observation, and even
The carcase downslope has clerically
Robed attendants loping to the wake
Among the undying asphodels.

Serious birds, the words to describe you
Should tap dance to a finger-snap,
For which of us is no scavenger,
Who barn the memories we forage
To keep us going when times are tough?

And at the end what could be kinder
Than their saraband for reminder
All too soon our descendants will spread
Nets out beneath the branches, ready
For the dark harvest we are leaving?

ALEXANDRA SASHE

pour Jean, tout cher

You are offered a wing
        of your left hand's
        emptiness,
        loosed strings,
        desireless surface.

You receive the offer with your
        rightwinged hand.

The daylight breathes through your lungs,
conductive of oxygen.

The name of the offering rests on your shoulders
        unburdened of all
        hide-and-seek names.

The straight line of your spine,
        your walking cane ever in blossom.

With the sun on your back and face
you stand in your own zenith. —

        The shadow-pointer under your feet
        shows the way.

Straying

Glimpsing again on
another smothered
morning—hot clouds low
over Heidelberg—
the tall blond student
who doubtless carries
sure as nonchalance
the avoirdupois
of a dustier
scholasticism

who I suspect's now
off to select books
(*real* books) which kindle
sparks of fact, complex
illusion and love's
enthusiasm

*who's unaware / at
his spring-age / that such
response / though lovely
must / belong alas /
to youth alone*

       who'll
stay nameless, one to
leave lodged in the past
like an expanse of
ordinariness, pale
water pocked with rain,
unforgotten

who
drifting from square to
square (not too near the
swirling Neckar nor
at times the Alph or
Styx) passes thirteenth-
century crannies,
cafés and a pink
church where Catholics
and Protestants vied
every Sunday to

out-sing the others
segregated by
The Reformation
and a makeshift wall
(petty but better
than roasting at stakes)

who might these days lack
religion bleakly
given examples
of intolerance,
bigotry and spite
(our fault who've tended
to treat naves as craft
grounded in dry dock
trendily missing
the mystical side
and lost the lesson
from soaring angels
who won't just jut like
their wood effigies
gilded or not)

                    I
wonder watching him
disappear among
coævals whether
he weighs what words may
be worth sung or read
haunted like me by
thoughts which don't often
lie too deep to get
written

            who may one
day sit toying with
a darker syntax
to cohere all that
he'd seen out walking
(or imagined he
didn't see)
            a red
bridge notched with flood-heights,
grave swan floating, two
profiles kissing, grey
garlic spread for sale
alongside roses,
unexpected tree
green against urban
stonework, street-jugglers,
window-flash

                into
a persuasive code
coloured as truth gets
altered to something
wider, wrings mundane
observance to show
shattered in sunlight

                23

what wasn't behind
it all after all,
waking surprised, fresh-
born, transfixed, to find
one's in a less non-
descript landscape where
iced horizons scoff
at proximity,
to-morrows turn their
backs on failure or
renown and letting
a certain quondam
callowness begin
advancing dauntless
into poetry

Rheingau, June, 2013

The Change

The relief!
While olive groves part along clean lines,
their leaves relieving the greys of stones, I

am relieved
not to worry that occupation...
not to have to worry that part of me

is shaken
like a duster out of a window.
The lower bole is leafless, windowing

groves of boles.
No hiding, no watcher, spine to bole
like a bud sealed against its own beauty,

figure once
fitted in me. Dove, don't bring a branch
to me, its brimful tiny vats uncropped.

Heathrow Lakes

Once at Heathrow visionaries saw
a flesh-thrown vase of darker matter

than the gravel pits whose moorhens, March
butterwhorls of marsh-flower, warblers'

bright voices, tone with planes, drone thunder
stop drone thunder stop. With swans and rats.

Thus my visitors, though waste, being
one mind, true bodies, each tucked inside

25

the other, asleep—these lovers think
they'll resurrect. They cast nets on spring.

And they question me, can your lakes clean
all this handmade muck from air, or flood

the traffic lanes that we've travelled? Yes.
Like calves skipping by the Reservoir,

ducks calling hark hark and following
floating sheep's wool, plentiful willows

straying from lakes along Coppermill
—when their panic is over, lovers

will decompose in me, as all will,
in water. Hail ditches, rain, or rest

in ponds in fields. Turn a million
lips on liquid swathes from Colne to Staines.

The Queen of Heaven in the Morgue

'That's not my son,' Mary said. 'Too young.'
Back in the drawer slid the black bag.

The river of blood was thick, crashing
attendants who overturned tables

damming stickiness. They were retching.
Another drawer slid from the wall.

Old enough. White hair, grizzling from black
skin. It was a woman. The super

said 'Sorry, this is wrong.' But Mary
gathered the plastic as if lightweight.

Before she reached the door, the viscous
emptying dried. You could see the floor.

Week of Flies 1968

A spray, 'Finito', was at our disposal.
We were urged to use it and not to crush them
against the walls or ceiling, to take care

to switch lights off before opening windows,
to excuse authorities for the success
of spiders escaping into our house.

'We must afford an invasion of insects
coming from the lake. They do not sting.'

I dressed in a black cloak. We swarmed unguarded
offices. Alsatians chased us and we lived
on free soup cooked up in Europe's cities.

*

With just one heart and so many nights
you mistake this cane for a camera
that stopped one foot from walking away

reminded it to end the wave goodbye
as if the trigger and flash that followed
were no longer moving —what you hear

is your hand clinging to this photograph
the way a map unfolds on a wall
to memorize how loose the corners are

—you limp as if the cane was adjusted
for distances, is carried too close
tries to remember what happened to it.

*

The hand that is too heavy
once lifted planes, suns
now wears a glove to a bed

that knows all about darkness
and the emptiness waiting inside
where your feebleminded fingertips

no longer can fold in
then yank as if a sheet
would open and just this hand

make its descent side by side
the warmth smelling from breasts
and afternoons spreading out

though now their sunlight
circles the Earth as ashes
—you pack this glove each night

the way a brace is locked in place
to hold on, take root
without air and now you.

*

This is it —a match, wood, lit
the way a butterfly returns
by warming its wings wider

and wider, one against the other
then waits for the gust to spew out
as smoke lifting you to the surface

—this single match circling down
half on fire, half held close
is heating your grave, has roots

—embrace it, become a flower
fondle the ashes word by word
that erupt from your mouth

as an old love song, a breeze
worn away by hills and the light
coming back then lying down.

*

It's not the sink —what you hear
is the sun all night calling its mothers
though their embrace still arrives

as thirst and the morning —two stars
brighter and brighter till the sun
is born at the exact minute it needs

to bury its darkness in the fragrance
smoke gives off as clouds and the longing
for rain rising from the sea —you splash

and between each finger its shadow
begins to breathe, is hugging you
with the wet towel and its hidden body.

*

This cup listening for shells is filled
and emptied as if the waves inside
are making room for the slow, wide turn

that won't let go —you drink from a spoon
dug in the way a fossil is pulled down
takes refuge as stone that falls by itself

—arm over arm you cling to the side
not yet the rocks mourners will lure
as shoreline sweetened with sea grass.

and though the table is wood it's trembling
circles down for smoke coming to life
where standing water should be.

ROSIE BREESE

Examination: Weather

Section A: Sun

1. It is scientific fact that an old man stretched out in raptures of sun-worship by a pool in Cyprus will eventually ripen as brown as a pod, so that you might expect his organs to rattle like kernels when shaken.

    Given this evidence, can it be argued that the sun is cruel?

2. Dust: If the sun was to turn its torch on you, and this torch was so bright that we could see particles of your skin as they were shed, would you say you were more or less human?

3. I wish to calculate what proportion of my body is a sly trick of the light. Devise a formula for this below, showing your working.

Section B: Rain

1. Assuming that under normal conditions a face will be mirrored by the droplets that fall in front of it, how many versions of you will appear fleetingly during an 8.5-minute wait in light drizzle* for a bus that you know you've probably missed?

2. If a droplet is capable of carrying emotion at a dilution of 0.01%, how long must I stand in heavy rain[†] before I feel nothing?

3. Is rain

    a) a tinkling of knives?

    b) a slicing of bells?

    Discuss, using real-world evidence to support your answer.

---

* Falling with an intensity of less than 0.20 inches (0.51 cm) per hour.
[†] Falling with an intensity in excess of 0.30 inches (0.76 cm) per hour.

Section C: Cloud

1. Is this a test?

Section S: Snow[‡]

1. If snow happens to be falling tonight on a hurrying crowd at East Croydon, is it fairer to compare it to dandruff, the crescent-moons of fingernails, both, or neither?

2. An empty bench, usually seating four, is refilled with how much snow?

3. "Every living person is tailed by fifteen ghosts." Discuss.

[‡] (With thanks to Arthur C. Clarke for question 3).

From a previous life

Speckle moon—what may you spill?
a rebel of sorts   paints a wishing well
on dry land   *in the middle is a large keep...*
pail   empty   as stockings
the morning after   *pain & cinders   fat goose fingers*
Mould   in the cooking pot
gruel in the casket   *there is washing to be done...*
each year   scarcely decorous   *nary nor kilter   riven & splinter*
delivers   scant   proceedings
Keep us from those   whose   knives/playthings/multiples
are stacked   fit to tumble   clay too
shall wither   *rib-spurge & kittens   dry root & brigands*
Such wont   such want   such wasn't
never having seen such lovely flowers

Simulacra

I minds moulds ... melancholia
laps infringes the boundary
between states stealthily it enters
gaining ground

The pit walls crumble
a house/cliff/garden succumbs to erosion tufts
of daisies daffodil clumps
cease to fulfil

reek & havoc

A figure turns a corner tends your way
one beady eye

recedes resembles converges

The table is laid for tea
the usual way escapes tentatively
representation

Something entirely else
lives underneath like the boy in the story
grown up overshadowed
by his former self

Plot

A taker of pains (no sugar)   metallic

wrapped   *sets-out-steps*

blueprint/layout/facsimile   *slender in its eloquence*

jacket ruched with insignia   rain

peeling/pounding   *night-plights nail-bites*

a book for colouring on the open table   *& the tree that sheds its leaves*

repasts of many kinds   *awash with hegemony & ergot*

(visitors of the 18th & 19th centuries are expected any time)

between now & noon calibrates connivers

the next day has away with words   *expectant the weather*

Sweet portfolio!   *seven-rags-to-rich-brides-dish-wives*

settling a part... swords at the hem

the mantelpiece realm   *cherry-trove pea-grove birth-pot thimble*

According to some observers

you are standing on the brim of an alternative

MARTIN ANDERSON

In the Year of Expeditions

"We are filled with homesickness for no identifiable home."
—James Hamilton-Paterson

Interlocutors of pure silences, and of snows. On a still night. What eye's afloat. What heart's adrift. Upon a fragment. A phantom.

From swampy, tide-washed wild flower salterns where the creek once bent by Lady's Island, poling with long oars up torturous narrows.

In our minds that 'implacable blancheur'; unmapped, untrodden. Illimitable waste. Flower of a cold lattice, on which the wave breaks.

Across the horizon History marches. Shadows weep. From the Archive of Paradise a rare bird. In its beak—exquisite plumage!—bright petals. We sought warmth in the ashes of their extinguished fires.

An expedition of vanishings. Air beaten to airy thinness. From the alembic of the Word flesh and bone excised. Each thing that we extolled we removed. A fragrance hung on the world.

At night in our dreams a strange figure came toward us. Then stopped. From the alder swamp by the dim light of the creek head it waved. It pronounced upon us all the blessings of whiteness.

And Joas Croppenburgh, and Giles Vanderputt, held back the sea for us. Day after day we heard, amidst sallow willow in the deep field ditch, it rage.

Over their ruined roads and villages only phantoms returned. With no memories.

Not even in the midnight cry of love tangling the high balustrade
—filigree fragrance!—does there float an uncontaminated moment.

Suddenly one night in our dreams she turned up. Unannounced. Forgotten. To claim, she said, all the gods, and all the songs, we had taken from her.

A new land, smelling sweeter than all the rest. The small boat we put over the side, to claim it. The exclamations of astonishment. What the wave brought back. The Chimera's gaze. The haunting artefact of loss.

In the penumbra's liquid throat. A hoarse aubade. Note flung out over settlements of stones and charcoal. A settled gloom. What ear, before dark, will hear that voice, before it is gone forever?

It is snowing. Over all the horizons of the dead the wind has fallen silent. The arquebuses dissolved. It is snowing, in the canyons of the blind where all the codices have been wiped clean. In the silence the pure fire of a crystal burns. No one leaves any footprints. No one arrives or departs.

Through damp backlands, where ditch side reed was in season, by old Dutch embankments, by steadings where hazel and dogwood loomed lush and full, by Marsh bailiff Zacharia Button's cottage, in the Year of Expeditions.

We searched for her. On the polluted tideway. Soured with salt. A wave breaking, always further off. Effigy. Rubbing. Our 'Ladie of the sea'. Slipping, always, from us. Scent, of that pure point-instant adrift on the word. That we pursue in our dreams. That our dreams pursue when we wake.

No journey's end. No end to looking. But under the moon we raised up a giant gallows. Harvested pain. We sharpened our blades upon them.

All the names erased—from plinth and citadel. The salt eaten into them. The vestige of a world returned to silence. They were 'Sojourners in the land' only. The un-cognised. Inheriting the Ocean.

The sea runs in us its incendiary course.

From the occluded depth of crystal in the steaming brine pan this sifted alabaster, asperged. Sea's lace. Sea's breath. Through whose freshet of lattices will dissolve, again, its unexpungeable vapours, endlessly protean phantasms and shadows.

Can you not hear, can you not smell these shadows jostling with their rotting cadence through a skin of depredations. Inscribed on the bones of the living, and the dead. Distempered, draped in a shroud. Entering the graveyard?

Murmurings, expostulations in the dark. But the orders have been promulgated. The street names changed. No evidence, no signs of a crime committed. All outward destinations are the same.

Whorled in the force of their going, torque of a name whose sound no longer exists except as another, deeply inscribed space whose signature is a wave alternating, overlapping, combining, upon which rises and sinks the inexhaustible flotsam of days.

On a still night, a sonorous chorus of birds. Roosting harmonies. Feather, moss lined dreams. The window's flickering lamp accentuates shadows within.

It is snowing. The air seeded with blossom. We stir in rooms above courtyards where the fountains have frozen. Stir to the shear cry of a gull driven by the sea's raging. A haunting cry wreathed in the high wrought balconies between sleep and waking. A cry reminding us of home.

When will the corn ripen again on the rises above the grey saltern's edges. Its shadow wave in the breeze. Beyond, above high perched Hawksbury, in the rain that falls without stopping, day after day after day. Where stalk and root rot in the ground and a malodorousness through the black earth continually oozes?

In the snow only the wind knows the names of those who are always weightless, who are always disappearing.

The thing about Grace and Laura

was that they were sisters, vice versas.
The gentleness of the one, tender
as mousse, flesh like marshmallow;
her demeanour like Turkish Delight;
an apricot mooning
at the sun; a salve for sore I.

The gunmetal slickness of the other,
her flick-knife wit and belt-buckle
tongue; operating from offices
in the City. I couldn't love
her. A wildcat, out of
control, she stalked me through winters.

Grace slides laughing on her birthday,
her soft haunches streaked with yellow
from tiger-lilies I've placed on her path.
Laura sucks in her cheeks and
intimates that, as per her email,
she won't be celebrating
anything in the current climate.

I edge away from her
coat-hanger glance.

If Grace and Laura were to marry,
that would be incest, anathema.
I covet a calling card for Grace
and she is always welcome.
Laura has me poked to bits
with reminders; red letters.

A Spat between Morning and Evening

Evening kicked up her skirts and span
seven times round the kitchen and laughed.

'There's a lot of the peasant in you
still,' said Morning peering over

his horn-rimmed specs, 'Sex
without finesse.'

Evening blanched, stung.
But continued to spin and flail

for all the world like a potato-girl
batting off blackfly with rags.

the path

in its bend to the right the trees disappear
down the pathway
                              you cannot see
the path but see shade from full branches
            sun shining on a hazel
                        in the foreground to the right
tells you where to walk

you will walk there later—in several days
or in a month or two
                              this path is overgrown
is hardly trodden now there are
            other ways to go from here
                        to another place other than down
and across on foot

for now you take in only the perspective
dwell only on how it turns
                              in full leaf
for in winter it is a different
            more open journey and you
                        see more beyond the trees
can decide how far to go

there is not this hesitation to fathom
such a pilgrimage on foot
                              where you cannot
see the way ahead but still go—
            once it would have been
                        common to explore the ground
ahead and decide daily

the paths now are straighter and wider
have fewer surprises—you
                            can see the future
arrive quickly from a long distance away
          no soft shaded bends
                      beyond which you may pause
before following the fall of the land

love poem with Cadillac

most think themselves in a game with competition
moves in the game consist of improvements
where it lasts for the life cycle

playing well means forming a strategy
within the game where there is always a question—
how to interpret situations

this is when the Cadillac can appear
an *idée fixe* that will never really disappear
if only to keep conflict alive on the surface

once identified conflicts can be resolved
hearts are broken when the Cadillac stops
conflicts are never suppressed or circumvented

no one can say how they will be worked out
but true love is when the Cadillac has gone

the mask

the wind is a mask for silence
it continues when the birds fall silent for a while
allows you to consider the concept again

for this place permits the thought to arise
rise and fall like an inland tide does not
crash and break on anything hard it encounters

sometimes approaches the purity of silence
you seek to hear   and fail
                    instead listen for sound

an inbuilt condition
                    hard to find fault with
listen in silence for footsteps that are never heard

your thoughts are illusions for the mask
that is included with no time limit for its removal

7 Haiku

pills
for Wednesday
more clouds than envy

shadows changing the length of day
hundreds of years
on paper

natives
fireflies not waiting
for complete darkness

sunrises since 1492
colored lines cross
the graph

early morning bird songs
not so strong to make the stock market
rally

dropping petals on our visit
—
the weekend's
famous cherry trees

museum shop souvenirs
Picasso's hometown
fame

Hands Are Better as Birdless Cages

I have a secret fear of being baptized by Mormons after I die. Some confessions are best boxed up and stacked in the attic—not the smoldering recent kind, of course, which would only make a tinder of the rooms you've carved for truth, but the old honesties left like dead begonias in the garden. Too heavy to lift and carry away; too sad to call ornament. Silence will be the first sign of the apocalypse. (My love for you, by the way, is like a taxicab with no driver.) It was not the rain that raised the gooseflesh on my skin but the way the light peered in and made a little film about dust's journey through history.

A Brief Guide to the Firmament

Fresh angels are terrible diagnosticians. You know the old saying: *The fresher the angel, the worse the prognosis.* It has something to do with their new noses, or maybe the way their wings push so much truth toward their faces. It is not easy to be a new angel. The technology of Heaven is decades behind. The only medical supplies are reserved for the harpists who slice open their fingers. The older angels, of course, can play chords in their sleep, and they do, so that all the halls of Paradise are lined with the music of slumbering ghosts. *Son, you'll understand when you're older* are words that are never heard in the afterlife. Also, *Do you want to get out here and I'll go park the car?* Small gallantries are unacceptable currency in Heaven. The valet says sleep, my angels. Sleep.

from The Anthrophony of Unfamiliar Landscapes
(Partially Catalogued)

ADDRESS (98 Via dei Cappellari)

I needed weeks to understand: flip the iron loops just so, so that the shutters don't blow closed. More days to understand the laundry left below the window was for me: extra sheets baked brick-dry in sunlight for me to gather and to fold. That is Rome; that is what it means to be away: A foreign tongue twines with mine, and I succumb. Or I say *no, I'll go. The biting ants and signs of Christ have grown too large.* Weeks pass. I don't need earplugs to find sleep, but noises still invade me from the street. Is that like Rome, its cobblestones, its refusal to be home?

AMPHIBIOUS

Long after your departure I could not release the dry finger of your smile from the lockbox of my brain. Every trap is not a turtle, but every turtle is a kind of trap. Every creature that spends its beginnings underwater spends its endings avoiding the humiliation of grief.

BED

The problem with sleep is that it takes too long.

DEPARTURE

I pack up what I cannot leave: The wind that caused the sun's delay. The spray of syllables for the bereaved. Funeral trains in a field of sunflowers—simple gold rewarded by the light. I steal a phrase as echo of the path I take to Keats' grave, chiseled praise below each cross: *My darling son. What would I give to see him smile again.*

DETONATION

The birds flew up with the explosion, so that the rush of wings was like shrapnel that only further flight could wrestle from the skin. The birds rose and broke the sky, deceiving my eyes away from any carnage on the ground. A breath-length moment for protecting the rest of the senses. But it was only the police, destroying something suspicious at the south entrance of the market, between the cheese shop and the florist.

ELSEWHERE

In the Argentina of my mind, only the fools are forced to cross the world's widest boulevard. How many pedestrians does it take to change the direction of the whistling wind? When I say face west, I don't mean Los Angeles. I don't mean Boise. I don't mean *pave a lonely path to Pretoria.* Did you know that the Everglades are in constant motion? Or that crocodiles have been spotted in saltwater pockets? Once, long ago, I pocketed you in the Argentina of my mind. A coastal mind. A carnivorous mind. A wreck of a mind circling the Southern Cross. A disappeared mind that approaches the foothills of the Andes, and then vanishes like shadows at noon.

FAMOUS

The way the ocean is famous for surviving a billion lightning strikes, illuminated as though illumination kept it together, rather than gravity and the moon's off-stage cues. The way the squirrel is famous at the moment a talon shutters its windpipe. The way a blue jay is famous because it insists on fame, because long ago it learned to mock a hawk and thus bullies its way toward fame the way a whistle bullies its way past pursed lips. The way the balloon is famous when it slips the child's grasp and gulps the sky, displacing the air above it with tenacious speed and violence, the way the air is famous as it tries in vain to reassemble.

FISH

I am a stranger here, says the stranger, raising her hand as a shield in the worn warm room. When I visited the Sistine Chapel for the first time I swam in that space like a fish, listening to the other fish grow louder and louder until the guards clapped their hands for silence. *I am not interested in your country*, said the stranger. The guards clapped, the fish quieted, but then the swimming began to roar again. It isn't that I feared losing you. It's that before I even knew you, I knew you were lost. The people are so kind here, it's like a disease. When I visited the Sistine Chapel for the first time, little fish, I looked for God in all the corners. Hush, fish, or God won't hear me pray.

INVISIBLE (Roman vocabulary)

Some things are the same everywhere: Fish in water. The imprint of teeth in the skin of fruit. The way I curl my toes in bed, shifting my feet to sleep. But I wear hunger loosely here. Wet graffiti seals my faith: *Anche lucifero era uno angelo*. Even Lucifer was an angel once. Facing frescoes above my bed, I memorize the cherubs looking on. They dare me to decode their malice, peering from the fade of paint. I fall asleep to their temptation. I wake to name my hunger shame. (Shame and hunger are similar. Use the same construction to indicate humiliation and the need for food: *I have hunger, I have shame. Ho:* the first person possessive. In my tongue we are not that brave.)

Gendered Poetics

—too large people in the room, she regrets being numerous
      she begins
drawing on passages of trueness, she declares a mood, a mode:
sunlight on vacant lots, her own back yard, making more money at the
      fading gate
      closing crossroads
shifting binary norms

She rejects being numerous.

      She begins again
the woman's body, she says, bodies in the text
forming sounds, like the lips of lovers

She wonders
dialectically
about her vulva:

imagines structural inhibitions that falter the ground work.

      She begins
translated problematic
      She describes
a nearness unlike bodily relation unlike preformed notions.

Her tongue hangs, followed by her poetry
and the language—darts and:

almost touching his arm in parts of speech
She names him
      nameless

With her eyes closed she'd know him, moving from stanza to stanza
his long pale fingers, dislocating sexual difference

but replicates
gravity and claims his weight

      She begins again
dissecting, quite skeptic.
She'd know him with her eyes open
closed
or struck out.
Inside is implied in poems two pages earlier.

Most austere: rejecting the name she gave herself
      She
renames herself He
and He escapes category
deciphered.

And nameless, like a leaf, floats on the surface

He, in an act of drinking it all in
finds me
      you
      thwarting readerly design.

He sips, swigs
conceptual austerity
and rejects the metapoetic;

existing only to provide opportunities
for tremendous isolations.

      He begins again
unpacking a notebook, a stick of lippy and cigarettes

his motives, partly prudential, are like the unfinished cigarette

HELEN MOORE

Our Daily Bread

On the restoration of Talgarth Mill, Black Mountains, 2011

Seed   crust   dense body   crumb—

   at lunar Lammas here on Mynydd Du
       giving thanks for water, fire, steel,
where reclusive springs rise,
   begin their descent;

atoms of hydrogen clasped by two of oxygen
   tumble through Cwm Dwr-y-Coed
      (Valley of Water & Wood),
       land of shorn Ewes, who browse behind the shelter
that Bracken fronds provide;

above, slate-grey cumulonimbus
   (streaked as if the Sun just raked out its embers)
sees itself as liquid plying glassy lips of stone,
   dark hairy mosses,
      falling strands of come;

and on, flight of rotting debris, bark, leaf,
      a sheep-skull white as the Moon;
here we sit to cleanse our minds,
   make empty kists of bone—
      back-to-back our bodies form
      a Janus box
         sounding upstream & down;

   in-breath, hum circling
      round wind-torqued Hawthorns—Birds drawn
       to the hearth of our chant;

and on past stands of late Foxglove
the pagan-hooded stems that venerate the Sun,
nod & even bow as it bursts through chasms
in the cloud, charming all the streams
which now make common cause

before precipice pours
into ancient woodland,
& trees cling to gulleys scoured for thousands of years;

here in Pwll y Wrach, torrents—
pressure-wash on mud-stones
carving beds, tables, steps,
dumping Stork-nests of wreckage;

but downstream, how the river shrinks,
spreads a laundry of silks
where Dippers come to peck;
marbles enigmatic patterns—water-light on trunks;
hush, as the air shimmers with Coal Tits' piercing *tisou-tisous*;

then through a tunnel-shade of Hazels
spitting nuts in its pools,
it tinkers down the valley
with Enchanter's Nightshade
as it serpents into town;

there, tripping over boulders, it falls again, again,
smoothes itself back out,
kneads the feet of stone houses,
bubbles by the lovers huddled on a bridge—
flirts with us, makes postcards,
recalls how it's changed
course,

                                    is autonomous
         yet willing to slip back in harness,
replenish the headrace
         (old familiar, a pleasant sensation)

lend its resource as onto the wheel the Ennig roars,
         fills the oaken buckets
         (slotted hands sparkling as the mighty wheel tips),

              rumbles the axles,
                    & deep within the mill,

                    the massive shafts which drive the spinning grin—
                              cogs, teeth
                    that turn the granite millstone

              where grist, rushing through its eye,
         is crushed   feathered into sacks:

         baker   dough   town fired up.

Hollow Allow Woods

Trees into limbs alerting what foliage spaces abide refractive
cancellations   but the loss only knowable in earlier measures of
subtraction   bare structure awaiting in the lessened beds its over-
pinnings   restipulating earth through its stranger woods

      chastened yelps of the en-
      tanglement cornering a
      void already pitched
      to another tang-
      ential fashioning

      tentative claws of trees
      overstay their timid
      pioneer straying

      maimed to a target of loss
      but affixed to a vesselling
      in siftable hard tissue

      instructive voids at a
      rote of desert seedling
      then climax dishevelment
      revisits ramifications
      straddling a blip of light

That the empty of stone is to be tossed toward a tree supplement,
no other interval than this   to be a local dent out of step with its
ground rock   defers to a null henceforward nil crushing   steer-
ing from a rod to fix things into sill   the escapade is slipknots in
trees filling out the prior drabness in dip   no concave this raw
once extractable, how trees flex their superadded seams toward the
off-glow of convexity

A stouter nudge is disenclosing stony vent   for rough para-loca-
tions of the sent away   is it a sunken site of the world which pits
against any product-transfer of vertical slightness?   or was it
too heavily dropped for that retrenching invocation?   the void
proffers an out-of-stance but has long since been cistern-heavy
with the shade-acute density of another need

        translatable squat nurture
        of thanked holes
        risking boles thinking erect
        amid unprotection's
        kneeling surrogate

        plunged arena of ordinate
        extraction, flanks hubbed
        not ridged, flatness
        of sink calibrated upon
        other flotations of
        profit removal

        insecurely sprung-from
        offers retention at a
        variable compass of attachment

Storm-lipped, sonically lean planking gainful across cushioned
stores of void   no replacement of lost stones according to such a
solo-absent remand   self-pinning micro-forest but as deeply into
the matting of recurrence   the good of browsing a wound cur-
tailed onto trees   ancient violence intimately definitional, pain-
fully implemental   tubes of wind-screw oaks in the dependency
grain adzed out of quarry   the most supplied wreath is a cloud of
seed-heads

Lightly inured at peak foliage to being wrapped in a foxhole   be-
cause there is no more burrowing into remnant stone than here
no entrance to the extraction source itself   which could arise only
from a revision of the offer, or have coped with being basketed out
of itself   no more stunt growths, having already elongated the pit
platform

        trees don't nest in the
        quarry but are the spares
        for a more maculate delay

        its very plunge already taken
        up, this is not openness ajar
        but a void in a shell not
        of its own making

        the loophole given sticks
        a forage flecked in scales
        of counter-serration that
        skies will crank whichever
        is crisper than emergence

A negative enclosure made negotiable by transit quantities of loss
but scratched at zero   such micro-abridgements short-root
towards the belated traction-trails of trees   the only aftermath is
what incoming trees do tail off from the subtraction—not covering
over so much as conferring a renewed leanness of ground   what
is exact to sky but its non-piercing   only apparently hewn in
what puts to stalk as topping the outside of this locus

inverted

There are stars in the grass. You feel these with outstretched fingers. Your nails root in the soil, tickling the soft bodies of seeking worms. Your palms flatten. Your toes spring skywards. Your wrists beat with pressure, your knuckles rise and fall like viaducts.

Your fused calves are an arching whip above your torso. Your pointed feet are a hovering scorpion sting.

You look the laced boots of your companions humbly in the eye as you recede, a scraping suitor, from their presence.

You are a diver. The horizon swallows you.

subliminal

Do not look down. You have no need of maps. The path is sinking sand beneath shallow waves. You keep the world on your left, the sea on your right.

This is the street. You simply feel it. At the corner is the abandoned grocers, shutters down. The sign is illegible; you do not need the sign.

You need no compasses. Your feet swim below you. You sense the quiet ticking metal of parked cars, the distant reversing of vehicles, the whirr of passing bicycle wheels.

You cross the street. Your ankles describe the inclines of curbs, the distinctness of grass and gravel. The house peers above a bib of white-pebbled driveway, fat-cheeked, pink, stippled.

You no longer notice how ugly it is. You no longer notice the yellowed newspaper against the porch glass, the abandoned milk bottles, the layers of weather.

You open the door, remove your skin, hang it on the coat hook.

retreat

Go. Do it swiftly, hand at mouth, marvelling. Do not look back.

Paper darts will rain at you, each point perfectly folded, the creases sharp, the words within sweetly plosive, seeking. Do not commit the shapes to memory, repeating them silently in the night, testing them on your tongue.

Go. Go before the fragile shoes shatter beneath your feet. Hesitate, and grind glass fragments with your heels, waltzing the crazed pieces into pebbles.

Stop, and you will find yourself kneeling at a grate picking peas and lentils from ashes, said from unsaid, truth from text. Unhook those tugging barbs, the tender tendrils reaching for your ankles, the slow ambush.

Go. Believe in the midnight carriage, the wheels carrying you to an absolute ending.

promenade

You expected to be part of it: a human tide swarming the shoreline. Instead you stand apart to watch the slow progress, the select following a slivered beacon.

The electric spoke is precisely a mitre's length. More or less. The sky roses. The sea is a patch of poorly printed crosshatch.

You would walk out, salted soles skating glassy waves. But the pier is shorter than you thought, its distant bulbous dome the disconnected dot of an i. An island.

You wait, faithful. The lights flash. You might have joined them, might have been a torchbearer. But there is no signal.

The air is chill and heavy. Your toes numb.

They do not call out for you.

You make your own promenade, humming home, a rattling goods van on the rails, *a thumb of rum and a warm bed. A thumb of rum and a warm bed.*

Inheritance

From the two battered boxes
the postman brings
I take the knowledge of stars for beginners,
a book with old songs, school reports
and the pictures of my wedding day.
A brochure of indigenous reptiles.

In a few minutes I have sorted them
in little piles, seeing before me
the shelves they used to stand in.
And in one arm I carry what is left
to the cellar.

In the chest half filled with letters
there is room for it.
Yet when I return I find
the *Divina Comedia*
still on my desk.

The boxes I will burn tomorrow
with the driftwood
we pull from the river.
And with the past beneath me
I will write now
what I remember.

Dirt pilot

You ring at dusk
From the border of an unknown country
With gravel in your voice.
Your enemies, you say
Have feet of clay
And you've always dreamed
Of flying.

In changing winds you chop reason.
There are people, you say
You left to love.
There are people, you say,
You killed
So they are with you forever
In your fever.

A hundred times the sun
Has scorched your wings
A hundred times your bones
Were shattered
But only the ground, you say,
Makes you afraid
Of falling.

Art is a line
Through snow-white clouds
Paradise a shadow
Moving over the sea.
And when the air releases you
You want to be the swell
In the water.

I hear the waves crushing
On the edge of the island

While you take off again
Towards the light
And I will walk my sandy shore
Like every day
Looking for pieces
Of flotsam.

The river

Glistening through the chestnut tree
You blinded us and beckoned us
With promises of paradise
And tranquil nights.

We stayed with you
And the verge, you said,
Was made by you
To carry us.

In the evening light
We cleared the banks
And when we rose
We saw you glide,

While the apple tree
Lost its bloom
To changing winds
And rising tides.

One morning then
We woke to find
The borders gone
The current drowned

The past afloat,
And in the depths
Our future lay
Torn by you.

This Missing Arm

Martine had an arm off. How would Martine ever get repaired? Thought Frances, she was never a looker, as it was, and relied on her second arm to make up for her lack of beauty. How will you ever get a man, or another job without it Martine? I have two legs and I can cook. You can't cook without your second arm because you will never control onions or slice carrots. You are so much less with one arm. I will find something that one-armed women can do and I never planned to marry. You are now enormously difficult Martine, not owning up to the disability one armed ugly women face. It is now twice as bad for you with your arm off and your ability to do so much less than the pretty, subdued, public face. I have a plan to hide my missing arm under experimental clothing made for women twice my size, no one will see my missing arm because it is not really there, and also unimportant.

The Rocking Chair

Do you think we have discovered a true relationship and if so which one are you? Are you the one in the rocking chair making everything move and am I the still one? What kind of art are you? Am I art? No one can actually tell me if either of us are painted or in a photograph because we are so realistic. This is getting in the way of me being true to you Martine. While you rock I am watching you think about saying goodbye and it hurts my feelings when you go so quiet. Will you rock with me Martine? Take time to think about the future of us. If at the end of the book your chair immediately stops, because it is written to stay this way, even after death, it is always sad, is it not?

The Death

Why do people die so long ago Martine? I have no date for your mother's death. This is because of cancer... cancer swallows time and we don't ever remember anyone's death a few years later. I am frightened that now you have one arm, and also no hair, you are nearly dead. If you die tomorrow, I shall argue five years later that it was after the Olympics, before Wimbledon 2013. No one would know this is true or not, because remembering you this way will be difficult.

Cézanne: *Still Life with (Red) Onions and Bottle* (1898)

Each stroke flies into the singular,
like disconnects, free accents on
the top of the cork and an
onion's base.
    The wineglass
stem, off-centre, too far right,
keys a drama of poles
and pivots, turning points;
the onion,
        central in its lack
of centre, unlike the apple,
less solid somehow in its layers
and skins and micro-layers,
in its known but unseen
translucence.
    To be grounded
like an apple, each onion
would have to spin in space.
The wineglass stem
a variant
    of onion shoots
and vice versa, elements
of a proposition reversed
as if each refracts each
and form needs form
needs form.
    And the bottle (left)
and the cloth billowing
off the table? The blown glass
says all is design, the cloth
all is feeling; the desire
for the sign, the sign
escaping, escaping.

Cézanne – *Gardanne* (1885-6) / Three paintings

Rue de l'Enfer
  but not Passage du Diable
is just wide enough
  for a handcart

in hill towns perched
  on, scrambling up, spurs
or mounts. Granite rearing
  out of the plain piles

the solid geometry
  of plain walls, orchre
variations, and red
  roofs, clinging on

in a pyramid brut,
  pushing a church up
into air's heat-heavy
  groundmass flashing

and sparking with
  phenocrysts
that are light's constant
  liquidations, where form

is facet is form
  in light's constant
liquidations,
  what three paintings show.

At the base somewhere,
  a Chemin des Colombiers
or Charbonniers,
  three pumpkins

on a low wall,
    floats keeping the village
lifted up to the sun,
    lifted up to the sun.

Cézanne: *Dans les bois* – 3 (1898)

Something is running
    through the blue woods,
        so blue, all blue,
    running away
from each stroke and dab
    catching at, chasing
        from left to right,
    right to left.

Light is running,
    time is running,
        through the blue woods—
    just when light's settled,
you move, and it moves,
    jumping from leaf
        to leaf,
    jerking the brush

from thing to form.
    Raw canvas is light
        breaking through
    or the brush firing
and missing or the blue woods,
    all blue, so blue,
        laughing, laughing,
    'your eye is nothing'

meaning 'your eye has it
    but your hand's too slow'.

Glenelg

Dun Grugaig, Dun Troddan, Dun Telve
broch-of-the-queen—and one each for her sons?

each broch's
a sounding chamber
portioning the river's babble
so let's roll Gleann Beag
up the Balvraid cow-track

is it there then
hid in the trees?
we've to gauge Grugaig
by following Iosal
down to the bend

the curved walls hint at
the twinned shell bottle-form
roof-beams at a height
my confused imagination
can't return

Troddan's stepworn cross-
sectioned scarcements
and slabbed lintels
rimmed with melancholy
thistles and pale grasses

Telve still bending
its trim tower
below Cul an Duin
each stone runs
the river farther on

over the glen
the hidden burn's shown
in a paper-tear of trees

  alder, willow, rowan, hazel

threading a soft vein
through the spruce regimen

these broken crowns
hidden by docks and nettles
thought's full of gaps
ground to chaff
in the broken quern

so close your eyes
and cover the wall-
tops with eaves
adding the bustle that flickers
round a big fire

The Singing Sands

Moidart, Arisaig and Morar

It's another day
to walk the strand
on Rubha Da Chuain
where every cap
could be a seal flipping

another day
to look south
for the lost wind

which will open the bay
to gentler weather

another day
when our shell-cult holds sway
in Chonzie's crown of razors
tucked in the fold
of his Thinsulate hat

another day
to sip dark tea
from the mussel's flared rim

another day perfection
dulls the shore's zonation
as we squeak the fine
white sands of Morar,
their dead silica so clean

another day to finger poems
for the tide to read
and erase
while the beach counts
over and over

another day
of salt water
without storm,
light shattering
glinting fragments

another day
the sea reaches deep
spray falls
and orange-shanked
littoral birds want mud

another day
it's all unfolding
under the fucoid wrack
quieting the dark
tidal wood

What is a mountain?

a mountain is what you go a long way round to avoid

a mountain is a walk into the unknown

a mountain is the crazy river's reason

a mountain is what's not worth having

a mountain is identified by its thumbprint of contour lines

a mountain is nothing without its skyline

a mountain is a zone of intransigence

a mountain can't even recall its own name

a mountain is where we realise how far short we fall of the birds

a mountain is where even the scouring glaciers had to admit defeat

a mountain is the last resort of extreme views

Elżbieta Wójcik-Leese

Nordhavn Offings

> 'In this way, when I write bougie and so evoke light,
> on the inside the Italian word *bugia*, which means lie,
> is "lunging" and attracting around it a darker semantic field.'
>
> (Jean Portante)

4 MAY 2011
today only the spilt glare
        signals the sea   *havet : morze*

5 MAY 2011
the horizontals care
        fully displayed
against the turbines and cranes   *turbiny*

7 MAY 2011
the blue underlined
        with emerald
            or is it turquoise   *turkus*

8 MAY 2011
lustre of the littoral
            underpaths   *of Polish*

∧∧∧

the white spotting of a whale
        ferry—breathturning   *my first language lunging*

9 MAY 2011
the right half of the harbour
outsparkles the left   *left for languages*

10 MAY 2011
two bulging lamps slowly slide back
                as the ship pushes forward   *Danish wedges itself*
                                              between Polish and English

11 MAY 2011
a sudden raft topped with
                                orange
        sits squarely midwater   *svimmelt hen over det hvide*

12 MAY 2011
mute wind turbines mill the
        haze on the horizon   *pijane ponad bielą*

15 MAY 2011
one turbine has stopped
                mesmerized
by the slate hulk tearing itself
                off the coast   *dizzy over the white*

19 MAY 2011
the punch card of portholes
slotted into
the row of S-tog windows   *Ord som flade fisk der flaprede*

23 MAY 2011
the golden streak clearly claims
                larger
                much larger area   *Words like flat fish that flapped*

24 MAY 2011
smeared in the rain drops
extinguished by the grey
electricity shack   *Bathing in a drop's quiet light*

25 MAY 2011
early morning, concealed by the red of the S-train
early afternoon, the red revealed in the rescue
        boat on the pewter waves   *Bader mig i en dråbes stille lys*

30 MAY 2011
                    shimmering flatness
waves resting to ripples
Monday-tired with
            their routine   *mig (my) submerged in English*

31 MAY 2011
one wind turbine scooping the warm
                        sheen
in the corner of
the train window   *me : mig : mnie emerging to breathe*

NOTES:
svimmelt…/ Ord…/ Bader … —Pia Tafdrup, 'Min Mors Hånd,' *Dronningeporten*
    (Gyldendal, 1998)
dizzy…/ Words…/ Bathing… —David McDuff's translation of Tafdrup: 'My
    Mother's Hand,' *Queen's Gate* (Bloodaxe, 2001)
pijane… —my translation of Tafdrup's Danish and McDuff's English into Polish
    (Copenhagen, 2011)

100

In Water

'The colours aren't blending' she said

Light froze. Sound was hidden in stone.
Wind held its breath. Two pebbles
Talked about a long-faded joy.
In the wind-lashing storm,
The lake envied the sea.
Time wiped away the stone's face.
The cloud was alone
Seeking its shape and place.
In an ancient volcano's silence
The woman raved "there is no sun."
The desert hid in sand.
A hammer-blow hit my brain
Spiders everywhere. Everywhere webs…

But where were your hands?

Fire Consumes Itself

I wipe away that vapour in me now

My hands left still in that thrum
My face volatile, expressionless

Your memories like smoke drifted off
Not even fire knows they're spent

Your voice, the past's trace in air
It cannot return to itself

Rooms with many doors open onto solitude
Flowers undress morning for themselves
Darkness itself sleeps at night

If Stone Could Speak

Stone is nature's silent witness, its patient observer.

Only stone listens to the worn-out stories of man.

Stone: the deep breath of history.

*

It looks with a naked face, without a mask.

The stone's ringing intoxicates the temple.

Stone is hidden by the goddesses' skin.

*

Stone says 'Beauty is fleeting', staring at flowers.

But still it suffers its silence.

Stone is loyal to man. It even waits for his death.

*

Stone thinks, without knowing what it thinks.

God insisted on stone's muteness, people's too.

Stone: the colour of waiting.

from *Banished White*

words arrive dressed in dust sharpened
however lit the grain mouthway
straightaway a sand or strangled mind is made
the stinging springs of eternal valleys opened
never given in dry ribs
and that it originates again
and that it takes the cord and leaves it hammered and defenceless
you win above those craggy eyes
the structure that of falcon that of silver

*

wherever goes the ash of the atmosphere against
the small stones become silent terrified wherein I cannot disappear
not even that hooking of the eye
the hand which waves for help
on the belly sinks into the current and touches itself
I have another oval which says horizon
when it's dry at the front of the mouth
same thirst of runners who drop out

*

each thing lines up in the smoke and then can't restart
how many times there was a fish to astonish the folds
in the circle each time secret
with less grand power the circles appear
the rush for the entire sculpture
frees the cloudy invitation to chains
and my sister comes by again and all whole
an inheritance of leaves to chew upon

*

having shaken the calendar of the plot
the wrapping rises then sinks
other birds I tarnish
to call it wax if the scrambling of feet settles
snow leaves the number of leaves always great
thing I drag in my pocket so you can look at the flowers
and whisper the statue under still eyelashes

*

you can't be the first liquid and that's enough
I was climbing
not to monitor the swallows
but to hear a trilling
to feel it pass through me
from a motionless stroll
in the evening of the past
everything here in a fist of women
with the men
all placed and squared over there
and fixed in themselves
framed uneven smoke

*

and last come the eyes

and all the colours are boats
on arrival
the empty star as if still all white
while I choose stone of
two feathers one will fall away

With Vallejo in Paris – while it rains

Huddled under a poem of Vallejo's, I hear
thunder and lighting roll by overhead.
"Some hullabaloo in the sky" the Indian corralled
in a Paris alleyway mutters dryly.
Furiously water booms off the armour-plated roof of the poem.
Abraham, I say to him, Can you lend me an umbrella, a slice of cloud
dry as a potato dumpling buried in snow.
I'm fed up with not understanding the world,
with being the lightning rod of suffering, from forehead to toe.
Someone's got to stretch out a hand to me,
I need some kind of tunnel
that won't just come up in a cemetery.
Tell me, Abraham,
how it's all managed to give birth to a poem
that's tough as an Indian's poncho
and, at the same time, a poem with its shoulder in it,
a bread-maker's poem, a stud-bull seminal poem?
I shelter, I hide away, I make myself scarce
behind the parapet of one of your poems
where, from above, I can spy on
the footsteps of hunger as they go out into the world
to eat emaciated people, devouring
more and more poor people,
a million million paupers shivering with hunger.
Listen Abraham, named Caesar like an emperor in a black toga
and crown of thorns, how's it happen that your poems are so filled with
        sadness,
when it never stops raining human misery, and we've twisted
all the heels off our old shoes, and pitiless water
soaks through the tears in our poncho?
What a laugh it gives me that you've got the name of a Roman Emperor.
From eternity you should have been called Abel or Adam, but Abraham's
        fine:
your dear mother once called you Abrancito and she'd say, son,

don't think so much, thinking's no use for poor people,
thinking's just one suffering more.

              Listen to what I'm telling you, Abraham:
I've met so much hunger in Paris I go to the Louvre to eat bread and
          pheasants
at a Dutch inn. I grab a pint of beer from a man out of Frans Hals
and gorge myself on the foam. I exit the museum cleaning my snout
with my clenched fist and say, When will it stop raining in this world,
when will they stop, stone after stone ricocheting off the roofs of the
         poor,
when will it rain corn instead of funerals?
And I grasp Chaplin's walking stick, lift up the collar of my coat and
         set out
in search of shelter, a refuge where I can let what's left of the
         weeping pass by.
I sit down to walk with the sadness and come here to my resourceful
         friend
and ask him to lend me a straw mattress to lie down and sleep:
for a century, no more, lend me one of your poems, a seminal testicular,
anti-hunger poem, a Vallejian anti-hate poem, give me a battle cry
stifled by fear of the jailer,
a battle cry in Quechua or Mandingo, but with a roof and a floor
to lie down and die, I should say and sleep,
I contradict myself, I wind myself up, I nestle in, return
to being a foetus in my mother's womb; wrap myself up and hear her
         Andean
grumbling and groaning:
in Paris there's no Aconcagua, and I'm going to make it rain on God,
on his own face, the suffering of all humans.

         Someone says *carcasse*
and I say skeleton. Even with his back turned you can see
he's weeping, but he lends the shelter of compassion I ask for,
and I lie down to die, I should say to sleep, protected by the armour-plate
of Abraham's poem, I should say César's, I mean Vallejo's.

Notes on Contributors

GABRIELLE ALIOTH is a Swiss writer who has lived in Ireland since 1984, writing and publishing novels, children's books, travel books, short stories and plays in German. She also writes poetry in English.

MARTIN ANDERSON is the author of a number of Shearsman volumes, most recently the chapbook, *The Lower Reaches*, and the completed prose work *The Hoplite Journals* (both 2013). A new collection of his poetry, *Obsequy for Lost Things*, is due from Shearsman in the last quarter of 2014.

GASTÓN BAQUERO (1916-1997) was a Cuban writer, whose *Poesía completa* appeared in 1998 from Editorial Verbum, Madrid. A selected poems has been published in the U.S.A. under the title *The Angel of Rain* (Eastern Washington University Press, 2006), translated by Greg Simon and Steven F. White.

JAMES BELL has published two poetry collections, *the just vanished place* (2008) and *fishing for beginners* (2010), both from tall-lighthouse. He lives in Brittany. His latest eBook is *By Shinkansen to the Deep South* (Poetry Super Highway 2013).

LINDA BLACK is co-editor of *The Long Poem Magazine* in London and has two collections from Shearsman: *Inventory* (2008) and *Root* (2011).

PETER BOYLE is an Australian poet and translator who lives in Sydney. His latest collection is *Towns in the Great Desert: New & Selected Poems* (Puncher & Wattman, Melbourne, 2013). Shearsman published his translation of José Kozer's *Anima* in 2011, and will follow this with his translation of the same author's *Tokonoma* towards the end of 2014.

ROSIE BREESE lives and works in Cambridge where, amongst other things, she helps to coordinate a project focusing on extreme weather events caused by climate change. She has had work published in a number of journals including *Poetry Review, Poetry Wales* and *3:AM Magazine*, and reviews pamphlets for *Sabotage*. Twitter: @rosiebreese

GERALDINE CLARKSON lives in Leamington Spa and has had work in this magazine on two previous occasions.

KEN COCKBURN is a Scottish poet and translator, based in Edinburgh. Shearsman will publish *The Road North*, jointly authored with Alec Finlay and excerpted here, later in 2014.

CLAIRE CROWTHER's first two collections, *Stretch of Closures* and *The Clockwork Gift* were published by Shearsman in 2007 and 2009.

MAKYLA CURTIS IS studying at the University of Auckland. She has had work in a number of New Zealand publications (Blackmail Press, *REM Magazine, Flash Frontier*), and is editor for *Potroast 'Zine* (www.potroast.co.nz) an Auckland-based experimental writing and visual media journal.

Ivano Fermini lives in Milan. Oystercatcher Press published Ian Seed's translation of his *The Straw Which Comes Apart* in 2010.

Alec Finlay is an artist and poet working from Edinburgh. His collection *Be My Reader* was published by Shearsman in 2012.

Harry Guest lives in Exeter. Anvil publish his Collected Poems 1955-2000, *A Puzzling Harvest*, and the subsequent *Some Times* (2010). Shearsman published his *Comparisons and Conversions* in 2008.

Gary Hotham's most recent collection is *Spilled Milk: Haiku Destinies* (Pinyon Press, Montrose, CO, 2010).

David Kennedy teaches at the University of Hull. He has three collections from Salt Publishing and recently published the critical volumes, *Britannia's New Tongues: Body, Time & Locale in British Women's Experimental Poetry, 1970-2010* (Liverpool University Press, 2013), with Christine Kennedy, and *The Ekphrastic Encounter in Contemporary British Poetry & Elsewhere* (Ashgate, 2012).

Peter Larkin has a number of collections to his name, two of which are from Shearsman: *Leaves of Field* (2006) and *Lessways Least Scarce Among* (2012). A new collection is due from Shearsman in 2014/15.

Mary Leader teaches at Purdue University in West Lafayette, IN. Shearsman published her third collection *Beyond the Fire* in 2010, and will publish her next book in late 2014.

Yann Lovelock last appeared in *Shearsman* in 1997. After that he largely neglected literature for his more socially engaged work, for which he received the British Empire Medal in 2012. Translations continued to appear, however, of Marianne Larsen—edited with Anne Born (2006)—of Gilles Cyr, with Patrick Williamson (2008), and of Serge Pey, also with Patrick Williamson (2011). Since 2012 he has spent half of each year as an art editor in Taiwan, working on Fo Guang Shan's 20-volume *Encyclopedia of Buddhist Arts*. While there he started writing poetry again, including the poems published in this issue.

Becka Mara McKay's collection, *A Meteorologist in the Promised Land*, was published by Shearsman in 2010. She directs the MFA in creative writing at Florida Atlantic University. Her translations of Hebrew fiction have been: *Laundry* by Suzane Adam (Autumn Hill Books, 2008), and *Blue Has No South* (Clockroot, 2010) and *Lunar Savings Time* (Clockroot, 2011), both by Alex Epstein. Her translations of the Israeli poet Shimon Adaf are forthcoming from Mosaic Press.

George Messo has three collections with Shearsman, most recently *Violades & Appledown* (2012), as well as translations of İlhan Berk, Gonca Özmen and the anthology *Ikinci Yeni: The Turkish Avant-Garde* (2009). Shearsman will publish his translation of Orhan Veli's *Collected Poems* in late 2014.

CHRISTOPHER MIDDLETON lives in Austin, Texas. One of Britain's finest poets, his *Collected Poems* (2009) and *Collected Later Poems* (2014)— which together collect all of the poems he wishes to preserve—have been published by Carcanet and should be on the shelves of all those who want to experience the best that modern English poetry can offer. The poems here all appear in the *Collected Later Poems*.

HELEN MOORE lives in Frome, Somerset. Her first full-length collection, *Hedge Fund*, was published by Shearsman in 2012.

SONIA OVERALL teaches at the University of Kent. She has published two novels, *A Likeness* and *The Realm of Shells*, both from Fourth Estate. A third novel, *Eden*, is in progress.

GONCA ÖZMEN lives in Istanbul, and is one of Turkey's most respected younger poets. Shearsman published her collection *The Sea Within*, in George Messo's translation in 2011.

SIMON PERCHIK lives in Long Island, NY. His poetry career stretches back to the 1950s, and Pavement Saw Press issued his *Hands Collected: Poems 1949-1999* in 2000. Of his subsequent collections, the most recent is *Almost Rain* (River Otter Press, 2013). He was a bomber pilot in World War 2 and, after attending university on the GI Bill, became a practising lawyer, before becoming Assistant District Attorney for Suffolk County, Long Island, in 1975. He retired in 1980 and has been a full-time writer ever since. His work has been appearing in *Shearsman* magazine since its beginnings in 1981.

PETER RILEY lives in Hebden Bridge, Yorkshire. Widely published since the 1960s, the majority of his work is now available from Carcanet (including *Passing Measures*, *Alstonefield* and *The Glacial Stairway*) and Shearsman (*The Dance at Mociu*, *The Day's Final Balance*, *The Llyn Writings*, *Greek Passages*, *The Derbyshire Poems*, among others).

ALEXANDRA SASHE lives in Vienna. Her first collection, *Antibodies*, was published by Shearsman in 2013.

IAN SEED has two collections from Shearsman, with a third, *Makers of Empty Dreams*, due for publication in May 2014.

HILDA SHEEHAN's first collection, *The Night My Sister Went to Hollywood*, was published by Cultured Llama in 2013. She won the Poetry Can award for her "contribution to poetry development" in Autumn 2013.

ELŻBIETA WÓJCIK-LEESE is a writer and a translator of contemporary Polish poetry. Her recent publications include: *Nothing More* (translations from Krystyna Miłobędzka, Arc 2013); *Metropoetica* (co-written with 'women writing cities', Seren 2013). The poem printed here first appeared in the last issue, but suffered from a number of printing errors and is therefore repeated in its correct form here.